African Animals Alphabet Book

Stanford Apseloff

OHIO DISTINCTIVE PUBLISHING

Columbus, Ohio

This book is for Evan.

I give special thanks to my mother, Marilyn, who spent her entire career teaching children's literature and raising four rambunctious children. And thank you to Glen, my twin brother, for the masterful editing.

Ohio Distinctive Publishing, Inc.
6500 Fiesta Drive, Columbus OH 43235
www.ohio-distinctive.com

Printed in the United States of America by
BookMasters, Inc.
30 Amberwood Parkway
Ashland, Ohio 44805
October 2010, M7918

17 16 15 14 13 12 11 10   7 6 5 4 3 2 1

ISBN: 978-0-9647934-8-4

Library of Congress Control Number: 2010913962

A is for Africa and **a**nimals too, all of them wild and not in a zoo. **A** also is **a**ntelopes in the setting sun. They pose for a picture before starting to run.

B **B** is for **b**ird, a spectacular one, a lilac-breasted roller basking in the sun. This bird is so brilliant, it does not look real. It has eight different colors including bright teal.

b

B

B is for **b**aboons, both small and large. The one in the middle is probably in charge.

b

B

B is for **b**amboo lemurs—fluffy, brown, and gray. The Madagascar forest is where they like to play.

b

C

C is for **c**heetahs as fast as a car. They are known for their speed but cannot run far. With this cheetah in front and another behind, how many spots do you think you can find?

c

C

C is for **c**rab with eyes sticking out. Its little claws pinch, without any doubt.

C

C

C is for **C**ape buffalo, with a lion lying low. If they see him watching them, surely they will go.

c

C

C is for **c**hameleon in the Namib Desert sand. The young ones are small—they fit in your hand. If you should wonder what this creature hears, the answer is "nothing"—it has no ears.

C

D

D is for **d**ucks, this flock in flight. Their feathers are colorful. Their faces are white.

d

D

D is for **d**rongos, black birds with a crest. They are high in a tree away from their nest.

d

D

D is for **d**og, the big one in front. These dogs are the best in an African hunt. This dog likes the jackal you see over there, and together they make an unusual pair.

d

E

E is for **e**agle, as you can see, soaring so high above every tree. With brown, black, and white, and a touch of bright yellow, this African fish-eagle is quite a fine fellow.

e

E

E is for **e**lephants, the largest of all. With their trunk they can make a loud trumpeting call.

e

F is for **f**rancolin with babies in tow. This red-billed francolin has three in a row.

G

G is for **giraffes** up to nineteen feet tall. These are the tallest land animals of all. Their necks are so long, they look almost absurd, and high up on one head you can see a small bird.

g

H

H is for **h**ippopotamus—what a long word. On top of the large one, you see a big bird. Unless you possess a good pair of wings, I suggest that you perch on more suitable things.

h

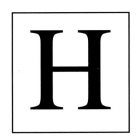

H is for **h**yenna, sitting alone. This little pup is chewing on a bone.

h

I

I is for **i**mpalas, which are smaller than deer. They are easy to spot with an M on their rear. These impalas lock horns in a challenge to test which young male is clearly the best.

i

J

J is for **j**ackal—look at him go. Where is he heading? I do not know.

j

K

K is for **k**udu—this is one of two types—with corkscrew horns and interesting stripes. This type is big, and it has a beard. I think it is cute, but some find it weird.

k

K

K is for **k**ingfisher, perched near a creek. It catches small fish with its very long beak.

k

L

L is for **l**ions lying in the grass. This one stared briefly but then let me pass.

1

L

L is for **l**eopards with spots galore. I count four hundred, but they may have more.

1

L

L is for **l**emurs of various types. Some are dark brown, but these ones have stripes.

1

M

M is for **m**onkeys who like to play, up in the branches during the day.

M is for **m**ongoose with a very long tail. I saw him up close, not far from the trail.

N

N is for **N**ile monitor, this lizard up high. He blends in quite nicely. Can you see his eye?

n

O

O is for **o**strich, the biggest bird in the land, fabled to stick its head in the sand. The ostrich is quick but too big to fly, and the bird has a brain the size of its eye.

O

O is for **o**xpeckers along for the ride. They eat insects and ticks in the animal's hide.

O

P

P is for **p**enguins on South Africa's shore. Go to Antarctica to see even more.

p

P p

P is for **p**aradise-flycatcher—a male. The females do not have this very long tail. You can tell from the name what this bird likes to eat—flying insects for sure are its favorite treat.

Q is for **q**ueleas, little birds in a tree. If you get too close, they will certainly flee.

q

R is for **r**hinoceros, big and strong. They each have two horns—one is quite long. These horns on their heads are a substance like hair but are hard and sharp, so you ought to beware.

R r

S

S is for **s**addle-billed **s**tork, I do say. It is graceful, I think, in its own special way.

S

S

S is for **s**tarling up in the sky. The bird flies away—I do not know why. The sun makes it shimmer in green and in blue, and sometimes you see some purple there too.

S

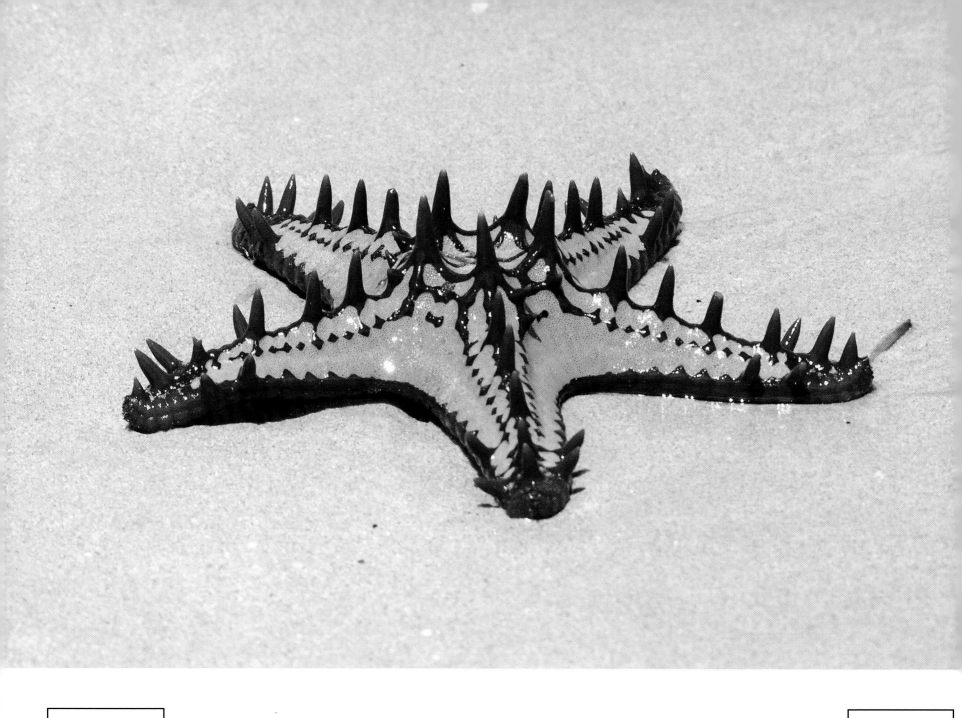

S is for **s**tarfish washed up on the sand. With bright red spikes, this one is just grand.

T

T is for **t**ortoise, our slow-moving friend—fabled to finish first place in the end.

t

U

U is for **u**mbrella thorn, a beautiful tree on a sunny morn. This tree stands over the giraffe below—see how the sunlight makes both of them glow.

u

V is for **v**ulture with wings so long. They are not very pretty and not much for song.

W is for **w**ildebeests, also called "gnus," pronounced the same as the six o'clock "news."

 **W** is for **warthog** who digs in the dirt. He uses his nose—I think that would hurt.

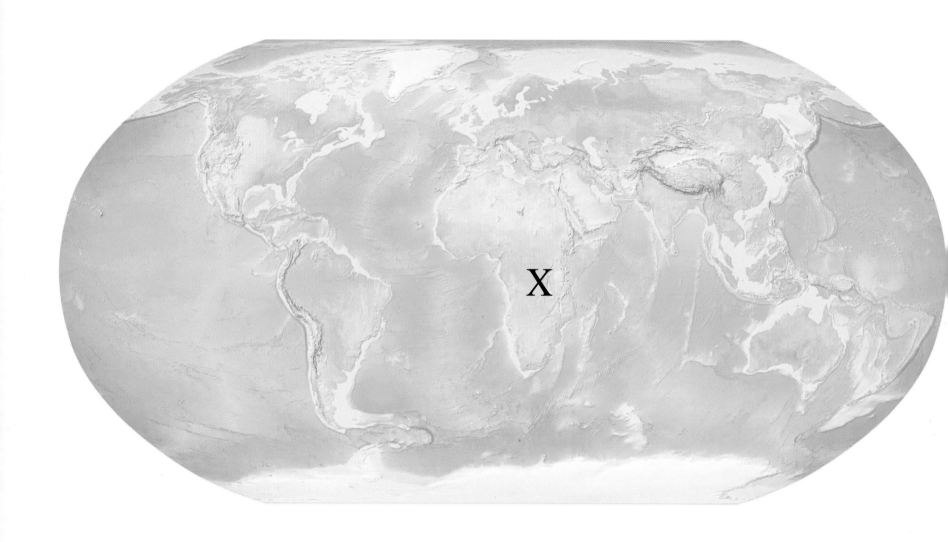

X is for **X**, like X marks the spot. Some words start with X, but most animals do not.

Y

Y is for **y**ellow-billed stork—that's its name. Can you tell just by looking from where the name came?

y

Y

Y is for **y**ellow-billed hornbills, a pair. These two face each other, and both seem to stare.

y

Z

Z is for **z**ebras whose stripes blend together. Riding along are three birds of a feather.

Z

And that is the alphabet with an African flair,
  with pictures I like and wanted to share.
I hope you enjoy this alphabet book,
  and venture to take another close look.

Read this book before going to bed,
  and the alphabet animals may stay in your head
And give you sweet dreams of lands far away
  until you awake to start a new day.

With each passing day and each page you turn,
  the more that you read, the more you will learn.